Creative Talents Unleashed

Presents

Unleashed

GENERAL INFORMATION

Unleashed

By

Creative Talents Unleashed

1st Edition: 2014

This Publishing is protected under Copyright Law as a "Collection". All rights for all submissions are retained by the Individual Author and or Artist. No part of this publishing may be Reproduced, Transferred in any manner without the prior **WRITTEN CONSENT** of the "Material Owner" or it's Representative Creative Talents Unleashed.

Creative Talents Unleashed

www.ctupublishinggroup.com

Publisher Information
1st Edition: Creative Talents Unleashed
CreativeTalentsUnleashed@aol.com

This Collection is protected under U.S. and International Copyright laws

Copyright © 2014: Creative Talents Unleashed

ISBN-13: 978-0990500940 (Creative Talents Unleashed)
ISBN-10: 0990500942

Dedication

With loving hearts the poets featured in "Unleashed" donated their poetry for this publishing to help establish a starving artist fund for writers that may not be able to financially afford getting published. All proceeds from this publication are being donated to said fund.

Please visit our website for further details:

www.ctupublishinggroup.com/starving-artist-fund.html

Preface

This book is NOT for the literary critics or the interpreters who sit as gods judging what is and what is NOT poetry or who is and who is NOT a poet! This book is NOT for those in authority or those that prohibit authority of expression thus the title **UNLEASHED**. This book is filled with joy, lined with heart felt questions, marked with pain and will take you on a poetic journey. We will take the reader on a visionary quest demonstrating we "All" have the strength to preserver and see what we see! After all, people do see with different perspectives.

Yes, there are sonnets to be found within these pages. Verses, stanzas, paragraphs and endings that rhyme. All the imagery and symbols that make up poetry can be found pressed upon the pages within, but what we, and the fellow authors of this book hope you will discover is. . . clear and accessible words with a language that speaks to you from the heart and maybe even alters the way you perceive the world.

Demitri Tyler

Creative Director, Writer, at Creative Talents Unleashed

Raja Williams

Author, Publisher, C.E.O. at Creative Talents Unleashed

Table of Contents

Dedication	v
Preface	vii

Jody 'Tru Story' Austin "Unleashed"

Humanity Doesn't Deserve Her	2
Pen	4
Human Struggle	5
Peace	8
Long Walks	10
Haiku	12
About the Author	13

Demitri Tyler "Unleashed"

[Census]	16
Tattered Flag	18
Dawn	19
Body Language	20

Table of Contents . . . Continued

Rites of Passage	21
Are We Done	22
About the Author	23

Shanese Whyte "Unleashed"

The Dread of Air Conditioning	26
Unleashed	28
Pensive	29
MJ	30
Collide	32
Tingles	33
About the Author	35

Billy Charles Root "Unleashed"

Poetism	38
Chainless	40
Letter to the Devil	42

Table of Contents . . . Continued

A Poets Dream	44
Line in the Sand	47
Tears in the Ink	49
About the Author	51

Elizabeth Esguerra Castillo "Unleashed"

The Hand That Rocked My Cradle	54
The Deafening Silence	55
Written in the Stars	56
When the Heavens Cry	57
The Phantom's Shadow	59
The Girl from Far Away	61
About the Author	63

Kofi Asokwa-Nkansah "Unleashed"

Left Behind	66
Friend	67

Table of Contents . . . Continued

Gone	68
My Poem	69
Dream Light	70
About the Author	71

Shelley Fowler 'Ajee Da Poet' "Unleashed"

Freedom	74
Done	75
I'm Letting Go	77
Open the Door	79
Butterflies	81
Isolation Scream Loudest In Solace	82
About the Author	83

Lindsey F. Rhodes "Unleashed"

Poker Face	86
Bad Investment	87

Table of Contents . . . Continued

Wal-O-Caust	88
J.U.N.K. Food II	89
Silent Cries	90
About the Author	91

Raja Williams "Unleashed"

Living in Loves Illusion	94
Katana	95
The Machine	96
Upside Down	98
Broken Mirrors	99
Time Keeps on Slipping Into the Future	100
About the Author	101

Stacey 'Eloquently Speaking' Lunsford "Unleashed"

I Am Large, I Contain Multitudes	104
Generational Curses	107

Table of Contents . . . Continued

Shattered Pieces	110
Behind My Anger	113
Fathers are the Backbone of a Good and Stable Home	117
About the Author	119
Starving Artist Fund	121
Our Links	122

Creative Talents Unleashed

Presents

Unleashed

Jody 'Tru Story' Austin

Unleashed

Humanity Doesn't Deserve Her

She has given from the depths of her soul
The fiber of her being to humanity
During its time of need
From a place of purity in its rarest form
Used and abused
Heart ripped and torn
Hurt and forlorn
Burned and spurned

Long stem rose thorns now poison
Bittersweet pain moistens her tongue
No longer the chosen one
Broken and misunderstood
Denial of the bad
She thought Humanity would make her feel good
She carried the world on her shoulders
Like proud soldier
True warrior
She cries out to the universe
Who is there for me?!
No one as far as she can see
Soul drained
Stained with nothing gained
Stressed and stretched far too thin
Weary within
Where then, is the humanity for her clipped wing?
Seeking affirmation in her King
Giving without an ending to her song
No wrongs in her righteousness
Virtuous in all of her endeavors

Unappreciated
She washed away the reality of her own reality

She came face to face with it and kissed it on its lips
Seen and experienced the cruelties
Her youth was stolen from her
No longer wanted
Tossed away
Gave freely of herself with no demands in return
Humanity never understood her....
Never fully knew the treasure she offered
Humanity never deserved her.....

Pen

Brewing
Chasing dreams
Calming spirits
Writing new life into the universe
Indigo dipped quill filling in the blanks
Night's companion
The paper
Upon
Ink
Spill
Letters
For the Gods
They free our souls
The words reigning from the heavens above
Brings us the peaceful balance on these sheets
For our freedom
Be power
Traces
Etched...

Human Struggle

We know that Humanity is a struggle
Within our community
And on these concrete streets that crumble
We must become beacons of light
And leaders of our society

Who told you that my 'hood'
Is the ghetto?
It wasn't let go
By my generation
And who named it so?
The meaning got lost in translation
Of those that confined
Demographics to jurisdictions
By those who don't know
Economic hardship
Or social restrictions
We must then move forward
To improve our conditions

My streets are filled with poverty
Subjected to gentrification
To line the pockets of the wealthy
In the name of low-income restoration
Who do they think they're foolin'?
Trying to create an optical illusion
Back door(ing) in funding
To remove us humans…..
From the equation
Of so-called run down urban areas

No jobs with no education
Keeps beautiful minds in a cage

Without a trade or vocation
It's a vicious cycle that builds
Chaos and rage
Followed by crime and violence that
Sets the stage

We must rise above
To break these chains
With work, faith, and love
And erase the mold
Dismantle the stereotypes
Daring to be bold
Eradicate the drugs and crack pipes
Our faces should not be pigeonholed
Into a profiled construct
And if they connect and check
Our royal history is correct
Let us etch
And re write a new
Biographical sketch

Surpassing all Isms
Investing in our community
To improve our conditions
One by one
Standing in unity
So much work to be done
Remove the drugs and illegal guns
It's urban warfare on our daughters and sons

Invest in our children
They are our futures

Be a guide as a mentor
To God's beautiful creatures
We must keep them in the center
It begins with them

To build their pride from within

When they can see
That they are the key
Within our tapestry
That we can overcome
That we can uplift
Equal parts of the sum
That they are the gift
Part of the solution
And not the problem

Only then
Can we improve this puzzle
Of what we call
This Human Struggle...

Peace

For everyone who is hurting
Lost anything
Lost everything
Lost another
A significant other
I will write a prayer for
Peace across my heart for you

For every orphan child
You do not deserve to be parentless
Be it from death or abandonment
May you never grow up feeling
Heart less, hungry, or
Homeless
I will write a prayer for
Peace across my heart for you

For every parent
Who grieves the loss of a child
May their spirit never leave
Your heart
I will write a prayer for
Peace across my heart for you

For every woman with
Low self esteem
May you build yourself up
And reach your dream
I will write a prayer for
Peace across my heart for you

For every homeless person
May your circumstances

Not worsen
May you find your angel
And be able
One day come off the streets
I will write a prayer for
Peace across my heart for you

For the over 50 million Americans
Who suffer from hunger
I hope my sister and my brother
Keep you
And feed you
For the 870 million hungry people
Of the world
The existence of humanity
Will be felt eventually
I will write a prayer for
Peace across my heart for you

For every service member who
Goes to war
May you return home safe
Sound, and accounted for
I will write a prayer for
Peace across my heart for you

For the serenity of
All man and womankind
I will write a prayer for
Peace across my heart for you

Long Walks

I want to take long walks
In the park
After dark
Embraced for hours
Claiming what's ours
Under the stars
Sharing laughter and long talks
Taking time to smell the flowers

Leaving blueprints on the beach
In the sands
During the night
With intertwined hands
Me staying close within your reach
Holding on tight
As I lay my head on your shoulder
Never far from one another
While we discuss gray hairs and growing older
Life continues to bring us closer together
To discover more about each other
The future is our buffer
The sweet things you say
Make my cheeks blush with color

You really make my day
The moon lights our path the entire way
And as we continue to stroll
We discuss our goal
Of one plus one equals two as our math
While letting go of the past

Ensuring that what we have will last
Securing ourselves by not moving too fast

We've stood the test of time
Never missing a beat of the others rhythm or rhyme
Imprinted in our mind
Because our history has been like a winding vine
Anchoring us like a lifeline
Leading us back where
It all began right there
Of the road map that led us
To discuss
What we are to be
And where we will go
Loving freely
As our feelings overflow

Under the constellations
We take a long walk
And find the future of our foundations
While we talk
In the park
During the day
Or after dark
As we find our way....

Haiku

Skies cry golden hues

God's painted canvas abstract

Peace after the storm...

About the Author

Jody 'Tru Story' Austin

'Tru Story' is a Registered Professional Nurse, for more than 20 years with specialties in Nurse Education, Mentorship, Cardiology, Oncology, Community Health, and Emergency Medicine.

She is also Retired Veteran of the United States Air Force 21 years in the Medical Corps, serving in Campaigns that include: Desert Shield/Desert Storm, Operation Southern Watch, Operations Enduring/Iraqi Freedom. Retired MSgt.

My mother was and is still a poet and artist who introduced me to poetry and expressive writing as a child in elementary school. My bed time stories were of Nikki Giovanni, Sonia Sanchez, Marcus Garvey, Phylis Wheatley, Langston Hughes, Paul Lawrence Dunbar, Chavez, Gil Scott Heron, Khalil Gibran, The Last Poets, and many others.

I was a classically trained musician in the earlier part of my life, and performed with different bands and ensembles. Coming from a family background of music it was in my blood.

My aunt was a jazz singer who performed with many of the greats that include Dizzy Gillespie and Charlie 'Yard Bird' Parker. There was always a jam session
going on.

All of these influences started my creative writing experiences as a child and throughout my adulthood.

My poetry styles are versatile in which I enjoy bringing a positive message. I participate in open mics and poetry/spoken word events as often as I can.

'This Is My Pen Vol 1.' Poetry/Spoken Word CD debuted October 4th 2013. I am in the studio working on my second poetry compilation and published chapbook projects.

Co-Administrator/Co-Founder of Family Poetry Collective (Philadelphia based poetry group)

Co-Founder of 'The Collective' Open Mic Poetry & All Artist Show at LaRose Jazz Club, 5531 Germantown ave, Philadelphia, Pa 19144

Demitri Tyler

Unleashed

[Census]

Ghetto
Barrio
Slum
Town

1. The left
2. The uncounted
3. The worthless
4. The down

Their
Big
Tall
Short
Small

Quite
Loud
Shy
Proud

Him
Her
Them
All

5. Twenties
6. Thirties
7. Forties
8. Old

Here
There
Working

Round

9. Machines
10. Tables
11. Floors
12. Piles

Until
the clocks
arms
are
tired and
sore

Until
the pennies
add and
a dream
can board

They know
tomorrow's
wheel is
the hamsters
chore

Hey!
Hey you!!
I hope
your writing
this down

Tattered Flag

I Am
star spangled in
tattered flag
a sun baked dream
just as beautiful and gracious as the others
though a slandered hand I've seen
I am ragtime attempting to alter the anthem of complacency
a fabled boy blue trumpeting for the pie stuffed melted pot
America she claims to be.

Dawn

At times it is not words
but moments that speak
to you with light,
embrace you with golden
ray, touching beneath your
flesh pulling back the haze.

As you slept my love, I
watched as the dawn eased
upon you, unwrapping your
delicate symmetry with, the
vivid colors of the day.

Body Language

I am in a room with no windows
just paper a pen and emptiness
with tongue pounding against the teeth wanting to say
and speak words into the wind
a heart with a longing to leave to crawl out of me
to balance on my sleeve
hands with the urge to pull free of my wrist to grab
crawl to hold
legs that want to run want to stand for me
eyes that dart in scan for the next opportunity
to be clear of me
that want to roll out of my thick dark skull
on to the floor out into the horizon they once knew
Maybe it's not a rejection at all
Perhaps the body's language for how it's missing you

Rites of Passage

I could be attached to a chain
at the bottom of the sea

I could be a runaway
with only a star to comfort me

I could be a series of
cruel jokes in American history

A shadow mourning the death of
It's body that died mysteriously

Could be an out of place African
note in an English song-

My tongue does not remember
my mind cannot recall

This poem could have been a
tear left to wallow in defeat

I could have been
Snatched
Stripped
Broken then
Freed

I am thankful for those
that came before me.

Are We Done

With horror and war
master king and lord
dog eat dog for more
race caste and class
that leave some of us last
religious righteous stand
nation colored flags
walls great and long
boarders spiked with thorn
history again and again

Are We Done

With egos hysterical dance
graves wide for mass
bullets in children's skin
embedded reporting spin
earth as whore to man
man as whore to oil
political punching bags
elephant faces and
donkey's ass

Are we done yet or do we need more?

About the Author

Demitri Tyler

Writer, orator and activist, Demitri the poet with the Greek name that if translated would read "dedicated to, follower of Mother Earth," is a rising voice out of San Francisco planting words of wisdom as if seeds beneath the flesh. His talents as a rapper formed his early years gaining him recognition as mc to watch in underground circles with performances at the Upper Room the cities hottest poetry/rap venue at the time as well as his activism in and around the community and state college campuses.

Family tragedy and the realities of life caused this man to hang up his rap career and vanish for over ten years but it was time well spent for out of the darkness has emerge a butterfly who has made the transition from rap to poetry look seamless, he is now teamed with and an equally potent force Creative Talents Unleashed where you will find his latest work, and is also where you can receive updates on his soon to come first publication scheduled for late 2014.

Demitri's Links

Author Page

www.ctupublishinggroup.com/demitri-tyler.html

FaceBook

https://www.facebook.com/demitri.tyler

Shanese Whyte

Unleashed

The Dread of Air Conditioning

The dead air stands still above my skin
drawing me in.
Seeping, polar kisses under the layers of flesh
boring holes of mesh with its tips of icy fingers
it lingers, deadly
threatening to overtake my body.

There is nobody to stop it.
It wants control, maximum hold
over the heat of my scarlet liquid

Insipid is the attitude of this air conditioner
that keeps me prisoner within its grasp.
I know it will not last
but eight hours of work seems like a molehill
turned mountain

That's something I can't bear to climb
especially when time keeps ticking...
slovenly.
This frigidity is agony.

I WAS NOT BORN FOR THIS!

It may be madness to think heat is bliss
but for once I'm proud of hot Jamaica.
If a genie said I should make a wish
I would switch this for warmth on any given day

Just to bathe in the rays that may
dance in little spots of cold fire on my skin,
see my blood melting
in preparation for the next day's pelting
of air conditioning.

Unleashed

Unleash the rains and wash away the pain
Of watching her fall for someone less
Than worthy of her kiss.

How could he but reminisce?
The sun's rays quickly ascend
As they bed the corner of obscurity –
Him being blinded by love –
Gracefully rising to dance on her eyelashes
Tinging gold her bronzed skin
And gently alighting a shade of a pink kiss on her lips
Never had he better enjoyed nature's gifts.

But whatever was this feeling within him
It had no right to take residence there
Even if her mere presence spurred it.

Pensive

Slowly slipping back to that place of suicidal solemnity
in which my skies are shrouded by darkness
it is silencing me with loneliness
and stifling me with sorrow
stretching my limbs at imaginary stationery
rapidly inheriting senselessness
swimming in my thoughts again

MJ

You beat in my chest
as I give over the rest of my imagination
to fantasies of you...
The truth of your innocence is sure.
I cannot endure the thought that
your person was, in reality,
so pure.
It is a mystery to me...

The way you sang melodiously
with no one being able to match
your harmony...
You are one with the world,
with human and earth's nature.
It is bliss to hear your voice kiss
the apparatus of ear...

I longed to have you but near enough
for a brush of your skin, your artistry, your ability
to move to the grooves of
magnificent music...
Music that lived in you.

Why could they not but see, merely comprehend the need
you suffered as you
called out for just one friend in this world?
For people to love each other, love themselves?
Why was it so difficult for them?
Just to love with a child's heart...

My heart aches continually,
breaks when subjected to your music...

All pleas for unity,
crying out, "PLEASE!
hear me..."

Collide

There is no music
Just beauty
Flowing peacefully out of you and me
In the quiet darkness.
Love like ours cannot again be harvested by anyone else.
We are bodies plush
The aroma of this love sifts through the air
As clouds that drift,
Elevated by passion.
We two collide forcefully
Causing a blinding electricity
That leaves us in awe of each other.
It is a wonder
How your soft lips and my tender body
Could create such a dreadful beauty.
The light that emitted from your eyes
As we reached our highest height
Reflected stars so captivating, so uplifting,
I could not come down.

I want to drift higher into Heaven with you.

Tingles

Have you ever sat still and felt
Tingles BURSTING up your sternum,
Choking you with surprise
As the memory of that somebody
Seeps into your mind?

Do you blush at the thought of
The touch he gave
And the responding tingles
Tickling your spine?

Do you then catch yourself for being so open
To the magic his words bring
As he sings promises
Of BRIGHT beginnings
In your ear?

And would you scold your conscience
For letting you succumb
To the tingles
Because you've had an underlying fear?

I too sometimes find
That in certain lapses of time
My concentration BREAKS
And his memory overtakes
All rules that my blood inscribed.

And instead of boiling fury

At the beautiful lies he told me,

This red liquid turns HOT as ice
As only the memories suffice
For the tinge of prickly sprinkles
Of ignorant puppy-love
TINGLES.

About the Author

Shanese Whyte

My name is Shanese Whyte. I am twenty years old and currently in my first year at the University of the West Indies, Mona, where I'm undertaking a degree in Literatures in English. I am an only child who found a new world through reading, and would experiment with writing idly before taking it more seriously in high school. I usually draw inspiration from random observances of the people around me and their behaviors toward each other. I also love to sing and often try to dance but I have yet to perfect my moves.

Drawing is also a hobby I have made use of whenever reading material ran out. However there is always a new book being written, new poetry penned and songs created, and so I am ever eager for a sample. I hope that I'll be able to influence my peers and even the younger generation to generate a similar passion for reading and writing creatively as I have.

I have had several poems published in the Jamaican newspaper, The Gleaner, between 2011 and 2012. These include, 'Pensive,' 'Lost Girl Inside' and 'Breaking Point', among others. This privilege has also helped in boosting my confidence to write more and share my writing with others.

Shanese's Links

Blog

https://viewsofawanderingmind.wordpress.com

Billy Charles Root

Unleashed

Poetism

po•et-
a person who writes poems.
Synonyms, writer of poetry, versifier, rhymester, rhymer, sonneteer, lyricist, lyrist;
a person possessing special powers of imagination or expression.
ism-
a distinctive practice, system, or philosophy, typically a political ideology or an artistic movement.

Ok here we go . . . .

A list of unreadable verbiage
Words with wings of humming bird flight
Spinning wheel of alphabet symbols
Starry glow hidden shadows light

Jumbled rhetoric shattered glass stained
Love lovely loveliness
heart on paper page

Slurred speech spilling mind
Dyslectic thought vision
Unseen sight with eye
Art of penning mission

Sights unseen within the norm
Every sight worded storm
No one thing void of form
Endless bliss raging scorn

Soul awaiting secret spark
Rising sunset setting sunrise

A thought within quiet dark
Creations cries.

Labor pains of the mind
Creating offspring emotionalize
Galaxy of thought planets align
Final push poem cry

And then
in a moment
All is clear
Focused vision appears

Itchy fingers search for pen
Hurry write it down
May never happen again

Releasing tension sigh
Nothing higher than this high
Except for the masters using I

Chainless

In the dungeon of Earth I walk weary
Dragging my shackles and chains
Praying Lord please won't you hear me
This hell is driving me insane
And who exactly strapped these chains to me
Must've done it while I was asleep
The weight of these chains is consuming
I pause in prayer and weep

I drag around the shackles of hatred,
for the chains that others drag around
I'd rather they all be shackled to me
And no one else be dragged to the ground

These links are so thick and heavy
They must weigh an eternity of pounds
While the clanking of the links of envy
Twist the drums of my near around

The shackle of addiction is squeezing
Against my skull and mind
Cutting off the spirits Appeasing
Of the chainlessness I might find

On my arm the chain of anxiety
That teases me wherever I go
And frightens me from propriety
And keeps me from doing what I know

On the other arm the chain of lost time
I can't go back even one day
The rust from the shackles is seeping into this rhyme
So what else can I say

Save me and set me free
Get these chains up off of me
I know that you have the key
So please come and set me chain free.

Letter to the Devil

I will not burn tho
I walk through the fires
I will not be blown tho
I stand in the storms
I will not drown
in my own desire
I will not turn
on a dime
And run away this time
I will not stay down
When I get knocked down
So put up your dukes
And let's dance
I will not take this
The lies that you feed us
I said out up your fists
And let's go

I'm tired of the hate
Tired of the lies
I'm tired of the story tellin
Backstabin and schemin
So put em up
And let's dance

I won't just sit here any longer
I've had enough this time
For The Lord is my Shepard
My savior redeemer
My shield

My strength

And
My light

So come on let's fight.

A Poets Dream

The poet sits all alone
on the floor
in a room
of his home
With pen and pad
Written poem
Box of writes
All he has to show
He writes of love
And pretty things
Of God above
And freedom rings
Push and shove
And dents and dings
With no one to lift him up
Alone he sings
They say his writes
Ain't that good
But his mind won't quiet
And his heart still floods
He has to write
It's in his blood
His dreams to publish
He set them down
His lips only wear
A saddened frown
Until one day
While writing in the park
A stranger asked of him
Is this seat beside you
A seat that's takin
He said no
Help yourself
And continued on

With his pen of felt
The stranger eyes
Glance for a peek
To see what was written
In blackened ink
The poet caught her
Out the corner
Of his eye
He tried to cover
Tried to hide
Stranger asks softly
May I please
Finish the read
What I read
spoke to me
Reluctant poet
With shy approval
Handed over his write
And said don't be cruel
She assured him
she would not
She took his pad
And began from the top
He watched her eyes
as they twitched
And silent reading
Of her lips
And then a teardrop
rolled down her cheek
Which followed her smile
and brought sweet relief
She threw her arms
around his neck
and squeezed him
Really tight
Stranger now
a sobbing wreck

Told the poet why
I'm sick and dying
From the cancer
I've been praying to God
For an answer
Shall I just give up
Or stand and fight
I saw the answer
In your write
I will stand
And I will fight
She walked away
New step in stride
The poet filled
With new love inside
Right then and there
He did decide
He would pursue
His dream set aside
If he could lift up
Even one more soul
He would fill he purpose
And be made whole.

Line in the Sand

Guilty judge the guilty
Before the king they brought
Caught in the act of her sin
Condemned to death they thought

Stones in hand ready to throw
The king inquired within
Guilty of death she is
For the type of sin she sinned

King bent down
Line drawn
In the sand
Question asked
To all retched man

Throw the first
If you have no sin
Cross the line
If you can

Stones fall
Accusers walk
King stoops down
For a talk

Where are your accusers
They have fled away
They are as guilty as thee
And have nothing left to say

Condemn you not
As far as east is from west
I've already forgot

Now enter Ito my rest

No one's sure
If he actually drew a line
In the sand of the earth that day

But one thing is sure
He drew it in the mind and heart
Guilty they knew while walking away

Tears in the Ink

A tear falls into my well
And the words come from life
There's a story I need to tell
Let me shed some light

Brewing deep within
Anger seeping into pen

Thoughts of hatefulness eat
Eyes drop tear into ink

Raging inferno of ridiculousness
Volcan-us erupt-us ness
High strung obnoxiousness
Behavioral unrighteousness

An absolute senselessness
In loss of common sense
Coagulated ink-less-ness
Till met by tear wetness's

A tightening vice on brain function
At spirit and soul inter junction
Causing hart malfunction
Resulting in
Outpouring of physical dysfunction

Tear falling slow in motion
Salty splash into ink black
Squeezing of pen choking flow
Scratching ball point commotion

Up roaring of flagrancy

Heart of fire
Wrenching angry
Burning hate desire

Malpractice in loveliness
Sinking pit of bottomless ness
Oh for the magic of calming kiss
But naught being hopelessness

Cheek rolling tear streak
Seeping sneak into ink
Pinching lips do not speak
Grinding teeth at the brink

Stay away
Do not come near
What I'll say and do
Is my most of all fear

Touch not my well
Of tear and ink
Touch not this well
Of my fearful think

Uncoagulated ink of self
By tears of hate for my self
War alone all by my self
This I cry my lord please help.

About the Author

Billy Charles Root

I was born William Charles Root October 21st, 1975 in San Bernardino California. For the most part I was raised by my father In Rialto and Apple Valley California. In 1995 I moved to Oklahoma where my wife Tina and I have nine children combined and three grandchildren. I have been a professional automotive technician for twenty years and am still employed for the United States postal service.

I've been writing since 2010, starting out with some short scribbles about my present spiritual condition. My writing became more poetic and revealing as I continued to grow closer to Jesus. From 2010 to present I would write poems and send them to friends and family. Then I started posting in various groups on Facebook such as "The Writers Connection", "Serious Lovers of Poetry" and the page "Creative Talents Unleashed".

In July of 2014 I entered a writing contest with many other wonderful poets and writers alike and won a five year publishing contract from Creative Talents Unleashed. While trying to put together my first ever manuscript I found myself tripped up by the loss of Internet and my poems being all over the place and completely unorganized while living the normal not enough time in the day life. I was emailing my pieces to myself on my phone while parked outside of McDonald's and Pep- boy's and wherever else I could snag a little free WiFi. Then I had to figure out how to use Microsoft Word to build the manuscript which was a wholly separate nightmare but I persevered.

As of September 15, 2014 I am an officially published author of my first book titled "Pressing On", I felt the title was fitting after what it took to get there.

Billy's Links

Author Page

http://www.ctupublishinggroup.com/billy-charles-root.html

FaceBook

https://m.facebook.com/BRootWrites

Elizabeth Esguerra Castillo

Unleashed

The Hand That Rocked My Cradle

Picture this, a mother and her adorable baby
With the setting sun at the background
She holds the tiniest hands as tears fall on her cheeks
Expressing the love for her child
Overflowing through the deepest core of her heart.

The velvety sky with tinges of orange, yellow at the far horizon
Mixes with the blue crystal-clear waters
Small waves dancing as if swaying to the rhythm of the mother and child's moment
As her feet touches the fine warm, white sand by the shore.

The mother's face is likened to that of a beautiful full moon in all its glory
Beaming brightly with each smile of her little angel wrapped in her arms
Oh, what a scene to see, a masterpiece can be created
In a single second captured by either a great artist's hand or through a photographer's nice shot.

Once, the baby grows up and see's this scene, she'll reminisce and utter
"This is the hand that rocked my cradle, what a wondrous experience it is to be born
With her as my mother, a beautiful creation of God, I need not ask for more
She has given me the best things in life and showered me with enormous love."

The Deafening Silence

With only the ticking of the clock on the wall
The tapping raindrops on the roof
The splashing sounds as they hit the ground,
As gray clouds hover over the gloomy sky above
Mind drifts to wander with thoughts of the distant past
A perturbed soul searching for answers,
The questions no one can even decipher.

The deafening silence puts me in a trance,
Makes me sail away to a different dimension
Trying to untangle confusing dreams,
That makes me lie awake in the wee hours of the night
Where am I? Who am I? Why am I here?
It is in silence that answers come rushing through,
When you can listen to what your heart is trying to tell you.

My mind is in a labyrinth-like maze,
Blinding lights chasing my shadow to illuminate my dark path
As I await for the Perfect Time when all these would make sense,
The deafening silence whispers his thoughts to me
Bringing me back to this chaotic reality,
My home is not here but in the heavens one fine day
When the Master up above calls me, then I can't make myself stay…

Written in the Stars

They say for each person
There is a certain Miracle from within
And you are meant to be just for one person
As time draws to a close to meeting the One,
The Universe and your Spirit Guides are on your side
To help you fulfill your One True Destiny.

It's written in the stars
And before you know it, I am coming to hold your hand
You may not know now but soon you'll get it somehow
I may have bumped into you along life's journey,
But you were too preoccupied with your own story
That you didn't notice me passing you by.

If in this life, we have to say goodbye
As my soul reincarnates, I'll meet you again in the next,
When our eyes lock as we cross our paths once more
You will know in your heart that it was me – your Destiny,
Just look at the stars on a beautiful night such as this
And know that the time is near to feel eternal bliss.

It's written in the stars
For even when True Love is lost,
Your soul will bleed for a meaning in your life
But though the inevitable happens, searching for your One True Destiny remains
If we are yet to discover our One True Miracle,
Even time may defeat itself in order for you to see me in another lifetime.

When the Heavens Cry

I have this fondness for the rain
Not just because of the rhythmic sound,
The raindrops make as they hit the ground
Like tears coming from the silent cry of
Someone we don't see.
A splash of shower, leaving a refreshed feeling
From a once dry and humid weather,
Like the dawning of a new chapter
Of your long journey to forever
Watering your path, leaving it alive once more,
From a once arid desert.

When the heavens cry
This inner child within me gets all mystified,
Eyes look up again to the high skies
Still wondering how this miracle came to be,
Just like the cycle of life.
When moisture is gathered by the clouds above
And when it gets heavy, it will shed tears,
'til her eyes run dry.

Rain…rain…rain
You are one of the wonderful miracles
The Divine created for mankind,
Do not pour out much
Just enough is all we need.

Cry…cry…cry
Little girl living in the vast sky,
Pour out your soul
'til your gloominess subside,
Let the tiny raindrops collide
And leave a magic spell,
On your once innocent mind.

When the heavens cry
It soothes this wandering soul,
Calms down my troubled mind
And all I can hear of is the melody
The music you create, dear Rain.
While others feel gloom
Seeing the gray skies,
My heart secretly jumps with glee
For I can see you once more,
My longtime friend, Rain.

The Phantom's Shadow

Through the dark night on a starless and pale moonlight
He lurks from behind, nowhere to go to
Just wandering the streets, hiding from the crowd
His sullen face masked
But beyond that scarred countenance is a dark past
That continues to haunt him down.
He may be aloof, be misunderstood by silly, shallow people
Deep down he has a gentle heart
Yet hardened by great blows he has yet to forget.

In each one of us is the phantom's shadow
Longing for more than just empathy
We struggle so much to find our niche in this judgmental world
To be embraced by all despite our frailties, shortcomings and flaws.
Why can't the world just leave him alone
And erase the stigma of him being different from the rest, an outcast?
Give him space to breathe, to live peacefully, have his share and prove his worth?

Through the dark alleys, there is where he hides
Hoping his day would finally come and can break free from the chains
Like any one of us all he wishes for is to find true happiness
And all he's asking from strangers is a little kindness
Every one of us long to be accepted for who we are
To fit in the crowd and not be left out

How do we bring forth peace in this world
When all we do is throw stones at each other instead of living harmoniously?

The Girl from Faraway

The silence surrounding her
deafens her aching soul
as she ponders on some distant thoughts
that continue to haunt her down,
a faraway look can be traced down from her mystic eyes
the look of a yearning heart
dying to escape from this wilderness she's in,
she looked upon the stunning stars from the heavens
as she lamented if she could just fly there to a castle up
above the sky.

Every morning, when there's a thick haze outside
Her mind wanders to a sanctuary
Only in her dreams she can see,
As she dreams on, tears come rolling down her eyes
Like dew drops falling in an autumn day,
The mind can't conceive sometimes
What the heart is secretly screaming out loud inside.

As she traverses hidden valleys and crossed
The high seas in every nightmare she weaves,
She dare not step in to a forbidden place in her past
A voice somewhere warns her not to go through that tunnel
once more,
And continue to move forward towards the light at the end
And so she walks on with bare feet touching the warm
ground
With robins and seagulls following her trail
While singing her a joyful melody together with the
Rhythmic sound of the splashing waves.

Alas! She finally arrived at her final destination
As a blinding light came flashing in,

Towards her countenance
Illuminating her whole being,
Giving her a calming grace
Touching her inner core
Soothing her aching soul.

"I have seen the light!" she uttered in deep amazement
And that was just the start of a wondrous life
She created again for herself
To be a living example of one who
Faced her own ghosts of yesterday,
Of one who have overcome
The dark moments triumphantly

About the Author

Elizabeth Esguerra Castillo

Elizabeth Esguerra Castillo is a Professional Feature Writer/CreativeWriter/Journalist/Blogger/Published International Poet and Author/Online English Instructor for Koreans. She is the eldest child of the late Roberto N. Castillo and Elisa E. Castillo, who both hail from the province of Pangasinan, Philippines, a province where a lot of creative and talented Filipino artists and writers come from. A graduate of Bachelor of Science in Business Administration Major in Management at the Philippine School of Business Administration in Quezon City, hilippines and another course in Computer Programming and Operations at the Systems Technology Institute in Makati City, Philippines. Her first two books are "Seasons of Emotions" and "Inner Reflections of the Muse". She has also co-authored more than 45 international anthologies in the USA, UK, Canada, India, and Africa. Elizabeth has garnered various international recognitions and awards. Her latest international awards include emerging as the Overall Winner of the "Winning Strategies Magazine International Awards" (WISMIWA), USA recognizing her positive influence to her community as well as to people around the world through her works and another glass trophy award as an "Inspirational Poet 2013" given by the PENTASI B Historical Forum and World Friendship Poetry Celebration held at the National Museum of the Philippines.

Elizabeth's Links

"All About the Love"

www.innerchildmagazine.com/all-about-the-love.php

"Inner Reflections of the Muse"

Now Available on Amazon.com

Kofi Asokwa-Nkansah

Unleashed

Left Behind

As the pleasures of this world overwhelm us
And the sorrows of the land caution us
Forget not, we are just passing-by
Just as the wind blows so is Life
It is full of joy and dust which sparks in our eyes to reality
Timeless as it may seem
As time bond, it is for real
Man's constant search for Peace lies right, in the Heart
For true peace, we have no idea of
Though blind we sing songs of Sight
For realms we relish deep within
Hoping to grab a portion
The truth of the inner man's passion
To be free and free in deeds
Never to be left behind
An act of Faith

Friend

Knowing you are listening, is all I care
Knowing you are there, is all I need
Enough says nothing but content,
Satisfied is not good enough a word
To tell you,
A friend gained I cherish
And one like you I pray to keep.

Hope to know what you know,
As I give what I have
For a common bond shared
Then I will say,
You are a friend
You are my friend
Thank you.

Gone

What I let go, I seek
Not the thing rather
its substance
Like the light of fire or
the hope it bright.

What I let go, I seek
Not the fame rather
acknowledging my existence
Like the jewel golden or
the rich yellow shine.

What I let go, I seek
Not the brawl rather
the chant of a Victor
Like Ali's "KO" shot or
the raw brunt of strength.

What I let go, I seek
Not love rather
a friend, one to trust
And care for unto death
Like nothing,
Just a True Friend.

What I let go, I seek
That is you.

My Poem

This is no poem
A write of words
Words of life
I seek no meaning
My thoughts I share.

This is no poem
You read these words
Words of light
You seek meaning
My thoughts I share.

This is no poem
This pen flow words
Phrases add to sense
There lies
My thoughts, I share.

This is no poem
This sheet it bears
Life it lights
So I share this
This is my poem.

Dream Light

A guide in dreams
A guide to dreams

Brightening our Steps
Shining our Paths

That Light above
Lights hope within

So we walk-on
In the dark

For the guiding light
That lights above
Truly shines from within.

About the Author

Kofi Asokwa-Nkansah

Kofi Asokwa-Nkansah is a self-taught Creative Artist whose works are largely; Poems, Quotes, Inspirational Notes and Digital Arts. His works are passion-inspired and often submitted online via personalized blogging sites and social media platforms.

He is free-spirited in the production of his works and tilts slightly towards being a non-conformer to strict guidelines of arts. Believing this holds much uniqueness for the creation of arts tagged as "Raw but Authentic".

For more of such works do Visit and follow his "Words & Pitches.

Kofi's Links

Blog

http://yarodmogul.wordpress.com

Shelley 'Ajee Da Poet' Fowler

Unleashed

Freedom

Can you hear it ringin'
I hear it singin'
Freedom
Opened up showin' me the kingdom
It's here that heaven
That number seven
Completion
Freedom
I'm runnin' towards the sun
The pain of my past is done
I have finally become one
With myself
No longer on the shelf
I know my wealth
It has not come to me with the use of medication
But through prayer
Meditation
Supplication
Even degradation
And separation
Have laid the foundation
Of who I am
A young woman
Who had to learn to stand
Right in the middle of God's unchangin' hand
Freedom
I don't know where to start
All I know is that it has taken up residents
Deep down inside of my heart
Freedom

Done

I now pronounce you husband and wife
Rice being thrown
I knew this was for life
Still yet newlyweds
You tell me this marriage is already dead
Not a touch of pity
Divorce papers laid before me
Not another word from you being said
Fears
The only sound to be heard is my tears
Landing on the typed paper
Pain like labor
What am I gonna do without my savior
The one who I savored
Is now telling me see you later
It must be another woman
Player
Leaving me the house as if you are doing me
and our unborn child a favor
With the shaking of my hand
I signed on the dotted lines
Longing to understand
Happy first birthday 1st birthday to you
As my son blew out his candles I looked up to see you
leaning on the mantel
Leaving me dismantle
I'm sorry Hun
I was too blind to see that you were my sun
Can we come back to being one
No longer do I want to run
Surprised
I looked my ex-husband straight in his eyes
You chose to leave your family for the streets filled with
fun

You can be in your son's life
But my heart is finally free from you
And we are done

I'm Letting Go

I'm letting go
Of all past pain
Things that have me hurting
Trying to drive me insane
Those who ridiculed me
Beating me down
Not letting me stand my ground
Those who wanted to rape me of my soul
Not letting me have any control
Those who treated me like
I was nothing more than mortal
Those who laughed and rebuttal
Those who felt my existence
Was taking up space
Not wanting me to be a part of the human race
Those who spit in my face
Hoping that the wetness would make my life erase
In haste
Told me that I was a disgrace
My mind replaced
All those lies
Those silly alibis
With the truth
They hated me 'cause they could see the fruit
That I produce
That's why they wanted to cut me down
They didn't want it to abound
But my feet have been planted on solid ground
See
I know now that without all of this torture
And pain
My life would have never been the same
It has brought me full circle
And created in me a miracle

It has taught me how to love
It has come from God up above
Through all the darkness
Stress and craziness
My life accumulates
My heart still glows
And illuminates
Even if they wanted to stop me
It's too late
To seal the fate
'Cause I already know
That will continue to grow
Because I'm letting go

Open the Door

One day I was looking out the door
I noticed a woman I hadn't ever seen before
She was in a dress
It was free flowing
Moving like it had a mind of its own
Not knowing
She was smiling holding the hem of her dress
So carefree without any repress
She was singing
Spinning
Dancing
She was romancing
Herself
It was like she found her true wealth
She was free
Wanting everyone to see
She had so much peace within
That it was blinding
To those who couldn't comprehend
I could see the glow of God shining on her face
She was in a place
Of contentment
No resentment
Just free to let all the love flow
She let her mind grow
Oh
I could see she was free from her woe
Drenched in illumination it spilled outside
I was so surprised
It was so bright
No more darkness of night
She let go of the fright
That lingered inside of her

She knew that she was more than a conqueror
With Christ that dwells within
He traded her a crown
For her sin
She was bold
No longer cold
No more full of hate
God sealed her fate
So blessed
No longer stressed
Free from being depressed
When I looked closer at the woman
I couldn't understand
What I had seen
This whole scenario changed from red to green
When that woman turned around she was me
So I opened the door and set my own self free

Butterflies

Darkness un-shown
Cocoon my home
No place to roam
Alone
In the lack of light
Struggles and fights
Through many unknown days and nights
I had no idea that one day I would take flight
To the highest of heights
Nature's plights
Billowing clouds of blue skies
Where I would rise
Resting on the canvas of God's painted flowers
Seeking shelter from the crisp smell of rain showers
Grand specimen am I
A glorious creation I can't lie
One in the number of many
Butterflies

Isolation Scream Loudest In Solace

My scream are loudest in the isolation of my mind
My solace has made me blind
A madwoman draped in intelligence
Smiling through my negligence
So many emotions have taken up residence
Fighting to kick them out but they are persistence
I'm covered in lace
Smothered by its taste
No longer wanting to emulate
But longing to regulate
All of my sorrow
Seeking a brighter tomorrow
Lord
It's so dark in here
The whispers of your light I hear
The soothing voice of your saying have no fear
I'm so close to you that I'm catching everyone of your tears
I'm washing you crystal clear
I have given you the greatest love
And that's the shedding of my blood
Take me by my hands
Of mercy and grace
And together we're walking out this solace place

About The Author

Shelley 'Ajee Da Poet' Fowler

Shelley Fowler is a author of a book called The Unprecedented Melodious Words of Ajee Da Poet, a collection of 64 poems that will make you think and see life in a different light. Her book is available on Amazon. She has also written poetry for two other books called The Necklace and Verses From The Heart. Both are in a compilation with other writers and poets. The proceeds for her poems The History of a Heirloom and Panoramic Orchestrations goes to support the Cancer Foundation in

Maryland USA to help cancer patients with non-medical expenses. Shelley is currently involved in a project called WINDOWS founded by Andrea Smith aka The Bionic Butterfly, the creator of ArtColab Grenada in Grenada. A few of her poems called Tunnel Vision, Significance, Summer and a few others will be a part of the show. They will be teamed up with painters who will create painting around her poetry. Jema Noel will be the painter behind the poem Summer. Shelley is working on getting ten novels and two other books of poetry that she created published in the very near future. You can reach out to her on Facebook and her email workwitwhatugotbaby@verizon.net. Shelley is native of Hackensack New Jersey.

Shelley's Links

Facebook

www.facebook.com/shelley.fowler

www.facebook.com/pages/The-Unprecedented-Melodious-Words-of-Ajee-Da-Poet-Shelley-Fowler/327716730674233

Sound Cloud

https://soundcloud.com/shelley-ajeedapoet-fowler

**The Unprecedented Melodious Words of Ajee Da Poet
Now Available on Amazon.com**

Lindsey F. Rhodes

Unleashed

Poker Face

Holding most of the cards to determine one's fate
Water-boarding, interrogation, and brutality is what awaits at the gate
Badgers and pigs running rampant throughout the street
While genocidal acts abound and remaining discreet
The republic is still standing yet remains on life support
Hunters hunting the hunted for the sake of sport
Poison in the well, dust on the crops
Phantom adversaries to the inception of photo-shop photo ops
Misinformation in HD shown all over the place
Playing the cards in plain sight in the midst of well-dressed poker faces

Bad Investment

Hopes, aspirations, and dreams were sold
Broken promises was what was told
Heavily invested with the heart as currency
All the eggs were in one basket; lost all of it both emotionally and physically
Fatal missteps hinging on the brain
Scorched from being burnt while praying for rain
Tapped out with no inkling of hope
Going through the motions; how can one cope?
A seller's market searching for the right prospect
Stagnated at the moment; time to change the subject

Wal-O-Caust

Gentrification in the form of low prices
The go to place in the time of crisis
Spreading false propaganda to ones who don't have a clue
Conformists united donned in khaki and blue
Started out innocent before turning into a festering pariah
Subtle hints to enter this global conglomerate through flyers
Warehouse of horrors under the rule of dictatorship
Casualties upon causalities reside on this sinking ship
Gatekeepers greet the naive with every arrival
Destroyer of communities; dependent upon them for survival

J.U.N.K. Food II

Mass distraction by design
Copious amounts of coverage; shifting the paradigm
Subdued by the slanted news
Taking it as gospel to dictate one's views
Stereotypical dialogue employed as doublespeak
Praying on the naive as well as the weak
1080 displaying catastrophes and misdeeds
Infectious appetite to fulfill misery's needs
Readying for seconds while licking the plate
Too much emphasis on "entertainment" with the remote ready to dictate
On what's important and what's not
The spell has been casted; therein lies the dark plot

Silent Cries

Real eyes realize
The broken promises and the constant lies
Living in a fantasy world albeit a fairy tale
Naiveté keeping the dream alive but clarity soon will prevail
Constant inquiries about my belonging
Outside looking in; togetherness is my longing
Depressed state of mind; actions are in slow motion
Ready to belt out and cry; no controlling this emotion
Learning to forgive and not forget
the best is to come but not just yet
Rising from the ashes of deceit for I caught fire
Ignoring those same voices by taking a road much higher

About The Author

Lindsey F. Rhodes

Sometimes the smallest step in the right direction ends up being the biggest step of your life. This is the very attitude that Mr. Lindsey F. Rhodes takes when it comes to new opportunities in life. Lindsey enjoys connecting with people through humor and life lessons. He has had the honor of serving his country and earning a college education.

Lindsey is the father of two beautiful children and raised four others from childhood. He is often asked how he can raise that many kids under the same roof and his response has always been "Time Management." His large family keeps his life interesting and thus in turn, a dull moment is never out of reach. Varying philosophies from each of them that can broaden an adults' perspective.

He is the author of CrossRhodes and a contributor to Love A Four Letter Word Anthology both published by Creative Talents Unleashed. This is just the beginning of his writing journey.

Lindsey's Links

FaceBook

www.facebook.com/lf.rhodesii

Author Page

www.ctupublishinggroup.com/lindsey-f.-rhodes.html

Raja Williams

Unleashed

Living in Loves Illusion

We claimed to love one another
But we were not truthful about our love
Our feelings based on sexual desires
And the meeting of our needs

We found escape in our loving moments
Filling our own, internal voids
Living in loves illusion
Something we tried so hard to avoid

Wanting to hold you close to me
To fill my desires needs
But our lack of true depth
Brings out jealousy

You break into a million pieces
Expectations left unfulfilled
When you're filled with envy
I cannot be your shield

Because I know the difference
Possessiveness and jealousy
Have no room in love
I hold you one last time

And I let you go in love.

Katana

Gentle rhythms
Silence the night
Cut by the blade of the sword

In one single swooping action
Everything cuts way to the NOW
A captured moment of freedom

Inevitable death
Performed daily in trance
Is the substance to the way of the samurai

10,000 arrows will not rip me apart
Nor will rifles,
Spears or swords

May I be carried away by surging waves
Thrown into the midst of a raging fire
Or struck by lightning from the Gods above

But to bring death upon a master . . .

I will die 10,000 deaths
Consider me dead
My soul becomes one with the sword

The Machine

With closed eyes we walk straight lines
Forgetting to open our eyes and dance in the intersections
We have become a living machine

Wandering through life looking for the connection
Missing opportunities because of lack of perception
We are driven by technology and its misconception

Forgetting to stop and connect all the dots
The machine took over
And has created the plot

Not able to bend and see the light
Lost in the illusion of the day-to-day grind
Being driven . . . by a one track mind

Break the shackles
And set yourself free
We are one-of-a-kind species, we are humanity

Connect with people
And create the space
Death of the machine we will celebrate

Because you and I, we are one
We dance in the intersections
The exchange just begun . . .

So step out of the machine
And take my hand

Together we will walk re-creating the plot
Time is relevant
Let's walk in the now
Death to the machine, that is how.

Upside Down

Underneath the push and pull
Polluted thoughts of right and wrong
Society speaking its terms aloud
Independents not a part of the crowd
Dependent on the need to provide
Education is what's keeping you alive

Darkened hopes and dreams
Oppressed by economic decline
Weakened at the seams
None the less, it's up to you how to get out of this mess

… Or remain upside down, in brokenness.

Broken Mirrors

Shards of glass hold fragmented images
While unclaimed darkness lurking in the shadows
Waits to cast judgments upon our rejected and disowned image

False projections cast reflections of unworthiness
Disclaiming our own greatness
With fear and self-doubt

Unconsciously looking in the mirror daily
Projecting ugliness with one's own thoughts
Dislikes running wild in a rampart playground of false ideas and beliefs

"I am not good enough"
Running truth in your ears
The projections of only, your deepest fears

Uncomfortable with the sight that is magnified and seen
Not a picture cut out of a beauty magazine
Righteously upset with the hand you were dealt

Angry,
Hypocritical
Nasty, the emotions you felt

Blaming the broken mirror for the image it casts
Close minded descriptions of your focal view
Your own self-image dissected right in front of you.

Time Keeps on Slipping Into the Future

I have come to realize
That before me lies blank pages
Ready for me to pen . . .

No matter what has happened in the past
With the breaking dawn of each new day
My future is always ready to be written

My tomorrows filled with all my dreams
Waiting to be created
Waiting to arrive at the scripted scene

At any moment I am able to be whom I dream to be
To create my future
And my destiny

So with this pen in hand
And blank pages too
I re-create this story

This very minute I make a choice . . .

And decide how it will unfold
Changing the central characters
And creating a new ending

Because this we know . . .

Time keeps on slipping into the future
And it's never too late to become
The person you have always wanted to be

About The Author

Raja Williams

Ms. Raja Williams, also known as Raja's Insight, fiercely arrived on the writer's scene in 2012 after being awakened by a prolific poet, lyricist, songwriter, and music producer whom encouraged her to write daily. After nearly twenty years of pent up words only floating in her own head she began to allow the words to spill out onto empty pages and find way to readers needing encouraging words. Raja entered one of her poems into a poetry contest and won a full publishing contract and released her first book *"The Journey Along The Way"* in January of 2013 with Inner Child Press. Through the publishing process and connecting with so many amazing writers and poets she founded her company

"Creative Talents Unleashed"

Having spent her entire working career in teaching and mentoring positions Raja found herself mentoring writers and walking them through the entire publishing process. Soon Creative Talents Unleashed moved from a writer's community to a publishing group. Within the publishing group Raja founded a program called the "Starving Artist Fund" to assist writers in having the necessary tools to become published authors at little to no financial cost.

Raja's Links

Creative Talents Unleashed Publishing Group
www.ctupublishinggroup.com

Website
www.RajasInsight.com

FaceBook
www.facebook.com/RajasInsight
www.facebook.com/CreativeTalentsUnleashed

Writing Group
www.facebook.com/groups/WritersConnection

The Journey Along The Way
www.innerchildpress.com/raja-williams.php

Stacey 'Eloquently Speaking' Lunsford

Unleashed

I Am Large, I Contain Multitudes

Being a black woman means
that I am large...

Being A Black Woman means

that I contain multitudes...

I am a daughter

I am a sister

I am an aunt

I am a mother

I am a lover and giver of life

Being A Black Woman means that I am a nurturer

I have the ability to care for my family, my friends...and my enemies.

I provide emotional, physical, mental and spiritual nourishment.

I encourage and inspire them to reach for higher heights...

I am an educator, a disciplinarian and a historian...

I am a black woman and I am beautiful....

Being a black woman means that I have the tenacity
to endure all kinds of stress,

all kinds of mess
and all kinds of weather.

Although the strong winds are blowing
vehemently in my face...still I rise!

Being a black woman means
that I am a Master Processor...
for I have learned how to appreciate
the process of being processed...

When they took my husband,
I cried but I didn't give in
I grew stronger....

When they sold my babies,
I cried but I didn't shut up
nor did I back up
I reached for them
I screamed for them

I became wiser....
I groaned with satisfaction
knowing that the good Lord
would be present with my children,
with my husband
and with me
eternally connected

I grooaaaaned with satisfaction
because I knew that some way
I knew that somehow...

the good Lord would provide
I knew that the good Lord
would protect us

I grooaaaaned with satisfaction
because the process that was designed
to destroy me built me up,
an evil plot that failed
I am not dead
I am alive

I am a black
beautiful woman
and I survived
I survived!

Generational Curses ~ Something Is Wrong Yall!

The prostitute out on the corner...
selling her body for drugs.
Her children are hungry
out on the streets robbing,
stealing, trying to get some food to eat....
Something Is Wrong Yall!

Their dead beat dad has flew the coop...
running here and running there...
tying to find a free place to lay his head.
He's living with another woman...
eating up her food,
running up her bills,
driving her car...
but I have a man is what she says...I have a man
Something is wrong yall!

Teenage boys & girls
having all the sex
in the world,
with multiple partners,
old and young...
venereal diseases
spreading,
fatalities increasing...
emergency rooms
Something is wrong yall!
and funeral homes
are full to capacity

Drug dealers on the corner...
infesting our neighborhoods,

bribing police officers,
firearms are spreading bullets left and right...
stray bullets hitting innocent bystander's
Mother is running her baby's been shot dead...
it brings me pain...Something is wrong yall!

Picture an iceberg in your mind...
at the surface that's all you can see...
but underneath the surface..
it's wide, it's deep
and it covers a large amount of the sea floor.

The definition of iceberg
is a large mounded mass of ice
that has broken away from a glacier
and floats in the sea,
with the greater part of its bulk under the water.

Underneath the surface something is wrong…
in the lives of our loved ones,
our families, our friends and our enemies
and like the iceberg is broken away from the glacier.
Many have been broken away from home, mom, dad, etc...
and are floating in a sea of hopelessness
and that brings me pain! Something is wrong yall!

Underneath the surface...I see strongholds that need to be broken:

Fear
Guilt
Shame
Incest
Adultery
Rejection
Depression
Pornography

Sexual Abuse
Mental Abuse
Homosexuality
Physical Abuse
Embarrassment
Emotional Abuse
Low-self Esteem
Child Molestation
Domestic Violence
Child Pornography
Inferiority Complex

On and on the list goes...it all brings me pain!

When will we find a cure?

When will we stop to care?

Shattered Pieces

If you see our "parents"...
Tell them that we "forgive" them,
Tell them that we "love" them,
Tell them that we "need" them,
Tell them that we want to be "whole" again!
Tell them that it's not about "them"...

Tell them that the first step
to restoring our family,
"is forgiveness."

Tell them, that it's okay
"if they" don't want to be together,
just tell them that we would like for them
to reach an "amicable agreement"
concerning "us"
and that we would like for them
to love, honor and respect each other
because it's the right thing to do!

Tell them that it will help us
to be come whole again!
Tell them that it will help us
to sleep better at night!
Tell them that it will help us
to do better at school
and that they wont have to
get so many letters sent home
advising them about our behavior!

Tell them that they have the "ability"

to change our situation
and to fix all that is wrong...
but it's not by their might,
nor by their power
but by the Spirit of the Lord!

Tell them that God is the only true "Soul"lution!

Tell them not to make us suffer
because of their "irreconcilable"
differences..."

Tell them "if" they want to be "together"
but the shame,
the hurt, pain, anger,
bitterness and rejection
is preventing them from
doing the right thing...

Tell them it's only a "distraction"
to keep them separated
and to keep
"our family"
shattered into pieces!

Tell them that family
is important to God!
Tell them that God
is a God of second
decisions and
second chances!

Tell them, that God loves them
and that "HE"
wants to help them!

Tell them, that God said to...

Come unto me,
all ye that labour
and are heavy laden,
and I will give you rest.

Behind My Anger

Behind my anger
is the overwhelming desire
to release the hurt,
the bitterness,
the resentment,
the shame
and the pain that I feel deep inside
I've been mad for a long time!
Years of anger all built up inside....
the lingering effects of slavery.

Behind my anger
is a strong determination
to release
what I am
feeling in a positive way
so that I can bring forth...
a positive change.
If I can change my perspective
I can change my life!

Behind my anger is an eagerness,
a willingness
to educate my children
my family
my friends
even my enemies....
about the lingering effects of slavery

Behind my anger
is a list of generational curses

that must be broken
but how can they be broken,
if they aren't being exposed?
My people are perishing
for lack of knowledge!

Behind my anger,
I see the big ships
that enslaved my ancestors!
Naked, hungry,
I see them in the spirit....
strong, they were very strong.

Behind my anger
I see the plantation
where our African American Men,
were programmed to drop
seed into his African American Queen,
than leave without bonding with his bride or his children!

Behind my anger,
I see that big strong buck being sent to another plantation,
to drop more seeds,
to leave yet another
African American Queen.

Behind my anger,
I see children growing up in a single household
because Massa Tom dun turned daddy into a rolling stone
Rolling, rolling don't know where he is going...
daddy was rolling.

Behind my anger,

I see the lie, (deception perfected)
and I'm exposing the works of the enemy.
satan I am going to tear your
kingdom down in Jesus name!
satan I am going to pray
your kingdom down in Jesus name!

Behind my anger,
I see hope!

Behind my anger,
I see the African American Queens
rising up in the spirit.
They are praying for their African American Kings
just like our ancestors did
when they transferred them
to another plantation!

Rise up my African American sisters...
rise up....
our African American Kings
need us to be strong!
Don't give up!
Don't give in!
Don't shut up
Don't back up!
Move forward and beyond!

Behind my anger,
I see the Lord answering our prayers!

Behind my anger,
I see restoration!

Behind my anger,
I see African American Kings
returning home!
I see broken homes
becoming whole...
all because his African American Queen
rose up in the spirit and prayed.

Will you join me?

Fathers are the Backbone of a Good and Stable Home

Fathers are the backbone
of a good and stable home.
I have been blessed
with a loving father,
who was also a
good provider.

With the help of my mother,
I have been rooted
and grounded in love.
That's a very special gift,
sent only from above.

For all of the times
that I have fallen,
my dad was there
to pick me up.
I am a single parent of three
and that certainly
was not what my father
had planned for me.

Falling off of my bike
and getting back on again.
Standing tall with confidence,
I hold my head up high.
Like the butterfly,
I am flying in the sky!

As leader of my home,

I have learned

that I can not be a
father to my children
because I am not a man.

As a mother,
I simply love
and nurture my children
the best way that I can.

The old fashioned way.

I teach my children that
if they make a bad decision,
make another one until you get it right.

For each new day that comes our way,
we have a chance to correct the
things that we did wrong yesterday.

God loves and forgives us this I know
because each new day that I arise,
my Heavenly Father gives me a make-up exam!

I am very blessed to have two fathers who love me so very much!

About The Author

Stacey 'Eloquently Speaking' Lunsford

Known as Eloquently Speaking, my real name is Stacey Lunsford and I am a professional single parent of three beautiful children. I am survivor of domestic violence and and advocate for victims of abuse. Creatively, created by the CREATOR to create inspirational and motivational messages through the artful skill of writing, web design, interactive media, image manipulation, audio, videos and music; paper and a pen are to me what a canvas with paints, oils and chalk is to Picasso.

Purpose of My Creative Works: At heart I am an encourager, I love helping people. Many people are discouraged, downtrodden and like a race car running out of gas has to pull in for a pit stop to refill, to be revived, to be rejuvenated and get back in the race, symbolically many people are like that racing car. My creative works are the pit stop, the gas provided for them to be refilled, to be restored, to be rejuvenated, to be encouraged and motivated to stay in and complete the race.

I've always heard the phrase that the race isn't give to the swift but to those that endure to the end and eloquently speaking somewhere in the middle of training and competing, life's circumstances get up in people's faces to distract them from finishing the race, many lose hope and they need to be encouraged, they need to be reminded that they have what it takes and that they can make it.

Humbly speaking, that's the purpose of my artwork, to declare that "Hope Is On The Horizon" by sharing inspirational messages of HOPE to encourage others.

My art is important to me because it's not about me; it's about serving and becoming the bridge to help others make it to the other side and accomplish their goals and be all that they can be!

Stacey's Links

Eloquently Speaking

http://eloquentlyspeaking.homestead.com

Hope Is On The Horizon

http://www.hopeisonthehorizon.org

STARVING ARTIST FUND

Publishing Assistance

In 2013 Ms. Raja Williams realized that there was a gap, a void if you will, within the publishing industry. A writer either had to come up with hundreds, sometimes thousands of dollars to release a book or take on the journey of self-publishing alone. There was no middle ground, no one there to assist, either financially or lead the way in self-publishing. Most writers do not have the finances to pay a publisher, and some don't know where to start when it comes to self-publishing, nor are they prepared to be in business for themselves.

Raja was inspired to start a fund to assist writers in becoming published authors at either a discounted rate or a full publishing scholarship. To begin this fund Raja paid for the publishing of our first anthology Love, a Four Letter Word. Comprised of poets from all around the world. The sales generated from the purchases of the book were placed into a fund that enabled us to fund future publishing's.

We now are able to offer anthology publications, a chance for authors to have a voice in the literary world yearly, and we have been able to offer several authors full scholarships, as well as offering deep discounted publishing services as a whole. We are thankful for the continued support of this program by both our readers and writers alike.

For More Information Please Visit Our Website At:

www.ctupublishinggroup.com/starving-artist-fund.html

Our Link's

CTU Publishing Group Website

www.ctupublishinggroup.com

Blog

www.Creativetalentsunleashed.com

FaceBook

www.facebook.com/CreativeTalentsUnleashed

Writing Group

www.facebook.com/groups/WritersConnection

Our Email

Creativetalentsunleashed@aol.com

Creative Talents Unleashed

Creative Talents Unleashed is a publishing group that offers an inspiring platform for both new and seasoned writers to tap into and participate with. We offer daily writing prompts and challenges to fuel the writer's mind, a variety of writing tips, and much more. We are honored to assist writers expand and grow in the journey of becoming published authors.

For More Information Contact:
For More Information

www.ctupublishinggroup.com

Creative Talents Unleashed

www.ctupublishinggroup.com

Creativetalentsunleashed@aol.com

www.ingramcontent.com/pod-product-compliance
Lightning Source LLC
Chambersburg PA
CBHW071514040426
42444CB00008B/1635